ROXIE MUNRO

BUSY BUILDERS

Marshall Cavendish Children

To Julia, Sandra, Vilhelm, Hugo, and Elsa

Many thanks to William B. Showers, Ph.D.,
Professor Emeritus at Iowa State University
and Fellow of the Entomological Society of America,
for his expert review of this book.

Library of Congress Cataloging-in-Publication Data
Munro, Roxie.
Busy builders / written and illustrated by Roxie Munro. — 1st ed.
p. cm.
ISBN 978-0-7614-6105-0 (hardcover) — ISBN 978-0-7614-6106-7 (ebook)
1. Insects—Habitations—Juvenile literature. 2. Insects—Juvenile literature. I. Title.
QL467.2.M86 2012
595.7156'4—dc23
2011017391

The illustrations are rendered in India ink and colored ink.
Book design by Anahid Hamparian
Editor: Marilyn Brigham

Printed in China (E)
First edition
10 9 8 7 6 5 4 3 2 1

mc Marshall Cavendish
Children

Insects are the most plentiful creatures on Earth.

Insects are the most plentiful creatures on Earth. They make up about 80 percent of the animal kingdom and live all over the Earth—in deserts, on mountaintops, in ponds, in the icy cold. There are about 1,000,000,000 (1 billion!) insects for every human being.

Insects can be helpful. They pollinate flowers and crops and eat other insects that attack plants. Caterpillars produce silk and bees make honey. Bugs like dung beetles clean up animal waste; others clean up rotting plants and dead animals, and many help make nutrients for soil. Some people even eat insects, such as grasshoppers, crickets, beetle larvae, and termites.

Insects can be harmful, too. Mosquitoes carry terrible diseases, like yellow fever and malaria. Beetles and caterpillars kill potato crops. Swarms of grasshoppers (locusts) can destroy whole farming communities. Termites and beetles wreck houses and trees. Each year, insects ruin millions of acres of cotton, corn, rice, and wheat.

An insect's life isn't always easy. To escape from enemies, some insects camouflage themselves to look like a leaf or a branch (bush crickets, bark bugs, stick insects). Many insects, like ants and wasps, use venom or poisonous stings as defense against enemies. Aegerid moths mimic dangerous hornets, which helps them escape harm. Certain butterflies and moths have patterns on their wings that look like the eyes of an owl—a big predator.

Many insect species live in groups or colonies, but few are builders. Some, like honeybees and African termites, work together to make their homes. Others, like the leaf-cutter bee or the garden orb spider, are solitary architects. The tiny builders in this book work hard and make some very odd structures. Can you guess what kind of home each creature will build?

FUN FACTS

- Beetles have the most species—more than 350,000 different kinds.
- Crickets have ears on their knees. Other bugs have ears on their head, tummy, or wings.
- Ants and wasps make up about one-fifth of all animal life.
- The largest butterfly, the rare Queen Alexandra, has a wingspan of almost one foot (about 28 cm).
- The green tiger beetle runs three and a half feet (1 meter) in just one second. It's the fastest bug on Earth.
- A huge dragonfly, with a two-foot wingspan, lived on Earth before the dinosaurs.
- Spiders are arachnids, not insects. They have eight legs, not six.
- The Goliath, the world's biggest beetle, can grow to six inches (15 cm) long.
- Butterflies are usually colorful, and they fly during the day; moths are often paler and are active at night.
- A tiny flea can jump about two hundred times the length of its body—more than twelve inches (30.5 cm).
- Dragonflies can fly at speeds over twenty miles (33 km) an hour.
- Many ants can carry more than twenty-five times their weight—that's like you being able to carry a car!
- Cockroaches have been around much, much longer than humans—almost 400 million years.

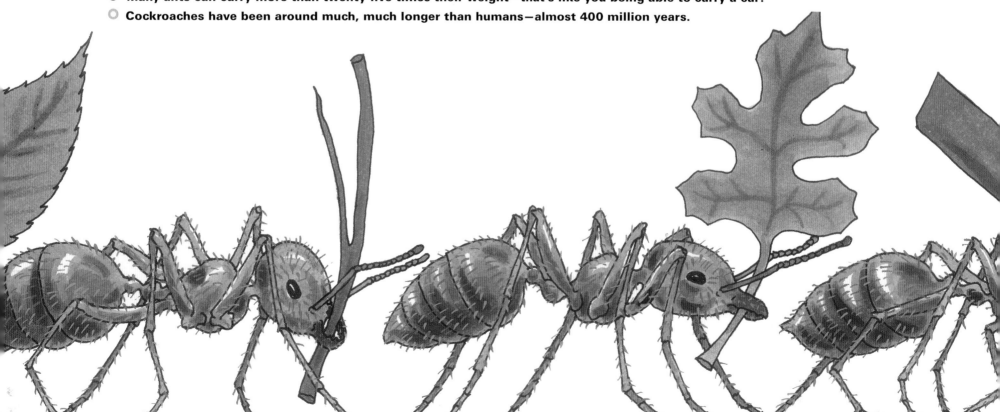

This is a **Honeybee**.

Where does it live?

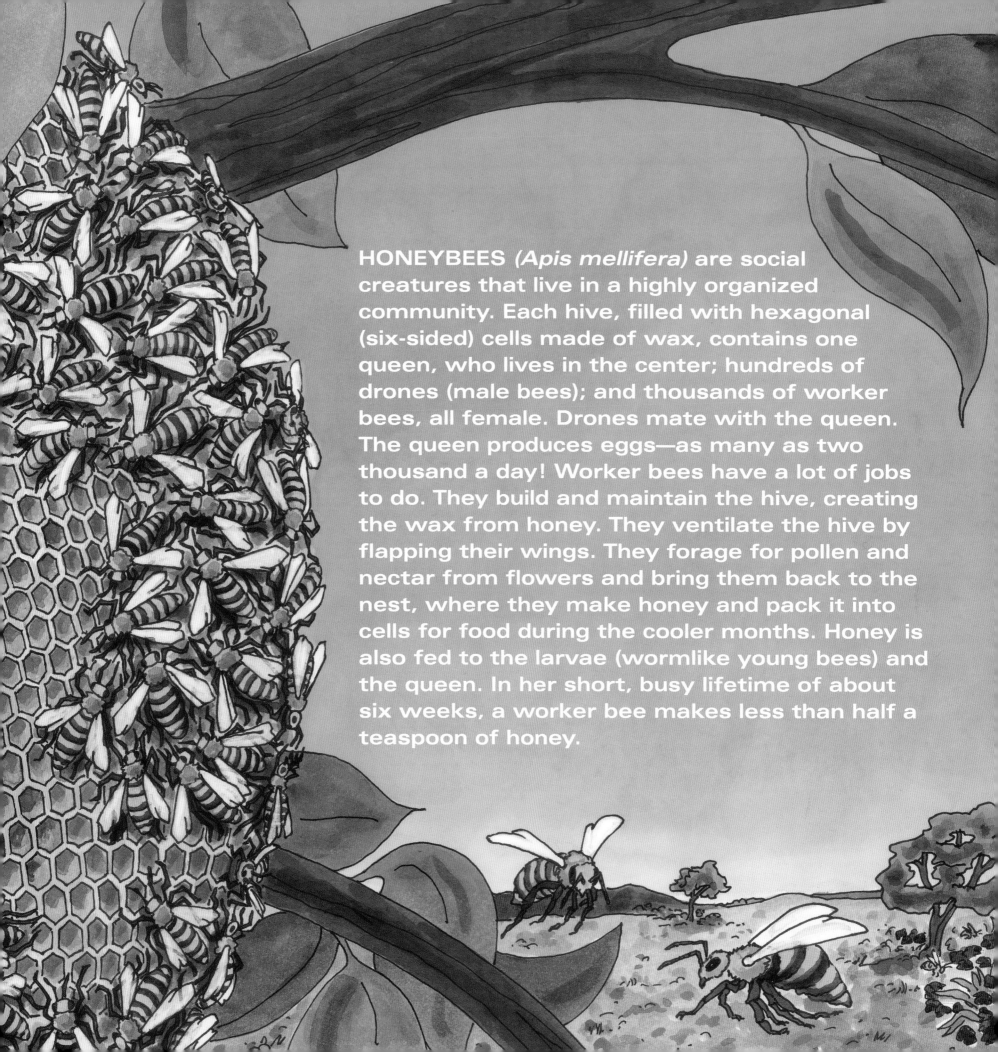

HONEYBEES *(Apis mellifera)* are social creatures that live in a highly organized community. Each hive, filled with hexagonal (six-sided) cells made of wax, contains one queen, who lives in the center; hundreds of drones (male bees); and thousands of worker bees, all female. Drones mate with the queen. The queen produces eggs—as many as two thousand a day! Worker bees have a lot of jobs to do. They build and maintain the hive, creating the wax from honey. They ventilate the hive by flapping their wings. They forage for pollen and nectar from flowers and bring them back to the nest, where they make honey and pack it into cells for food during the cooler months. Honey is also fed to the larvae (wormlike young bees) and the queen. In her short, busy lifetime of about six weeks, a worker bee makes less than half a teaspoon of honey.

This is a **Red Harvester Ant**.

Where does it live?

Long lines of RED HARVESTER ANTS *(Pogonomyrmex barbatus)* scurry back and forth from their nest, carrying seeds, grains, or leaves often bigger than they are. Over time, these ants clear the vegetation surrounding their nest, leaving a large circular patch of bare ground around it. Harvester ants carry their food through a single entrance hole and down into the intricate underground network of corridors and special chambers that they call home. Here, everything is well organized. One chamber is carved out for the queen; there are others for food storage, mainly seeds. There are nurseries and even special rooms for trash. Worker ants maintain the nest. Patrol ants are stationed at the entrance, while other ants go out to forage for food. One harvester ant nest reportedly extended fifteen feet (4.6 m) below the ground and contained 436 chambers.

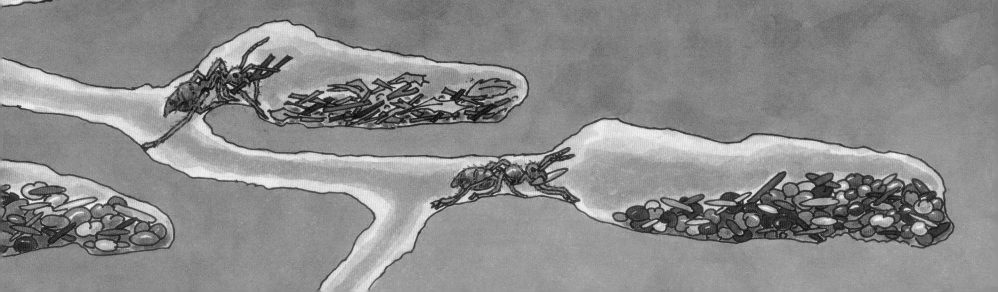

This is an **Organ-Pipe Mud Dauber**.

Where does it live?

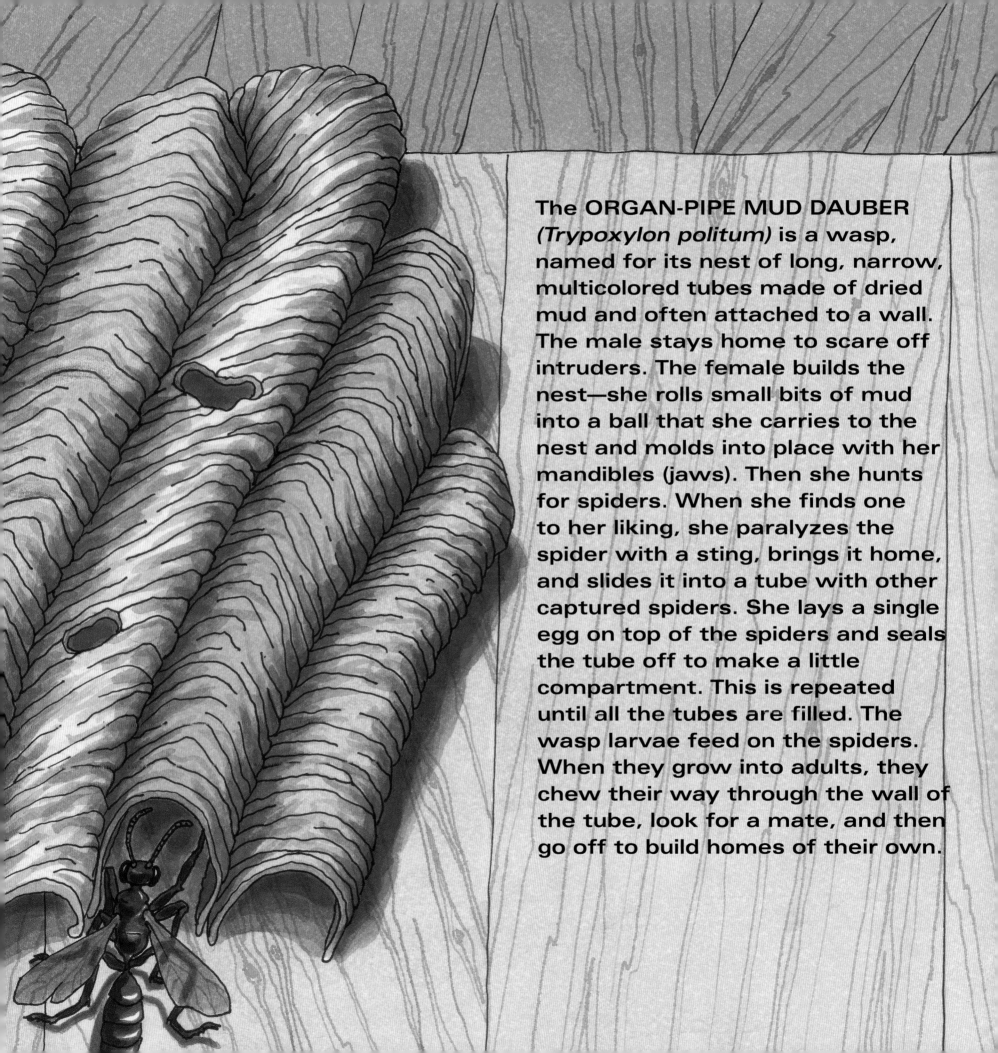

The **ORGAN-PIPE MUD DAUBER** (*Trypoxylon politum*) is a wasp, named for its nest of long, narrow, multicolored tubes made of dried mud and often attached to a wall. The male stays home to scare off intruders. The female builds the nest—she rolls small bits of mud into a ball that she carries to the nest and molds into place with her mandibles (jaws). Then she hunts for spiders. When she finds one to her liking, she paralyzes the spider with a sting, brings it home, and slides it into a tube with other captured spiders. She lays a single egg on top of the spiders and seals the tube off to make a little compartment. This is repeated until all the tubes are filled. The wasp larvae feed on the spiders. When they grow into adults, they chew their way through the wall of the tube, look for a mate, and then go off to build homes of their own.

This is a **Garden Orb Spider**.

Where does it live?

An insect that wanders into the sticky threads of a GARDEN ORB SPIDER *(Araneus diadematus)* web can expect to be stunned by a quick bite and then wrapped in silk. The image here shows a dragonfly that was just caught (top-right) as well as a wrapped fly (inset). Orb spiders build their webs in trees and bushes located in fields or forests. The web itself is an engineering feat. The spider floats a silk line from one surface to another (often tree branches), making a Y, then adds other lines. Finally, starting at the center, the spider spirals out with new threads until the web is completed. A thread of spider silk is much stronger than steel of the same width and length. The spider devours the web at the end of the day, only to build another one an hour later.

This is an **Australian Weaver Ant**.

Where does it live?

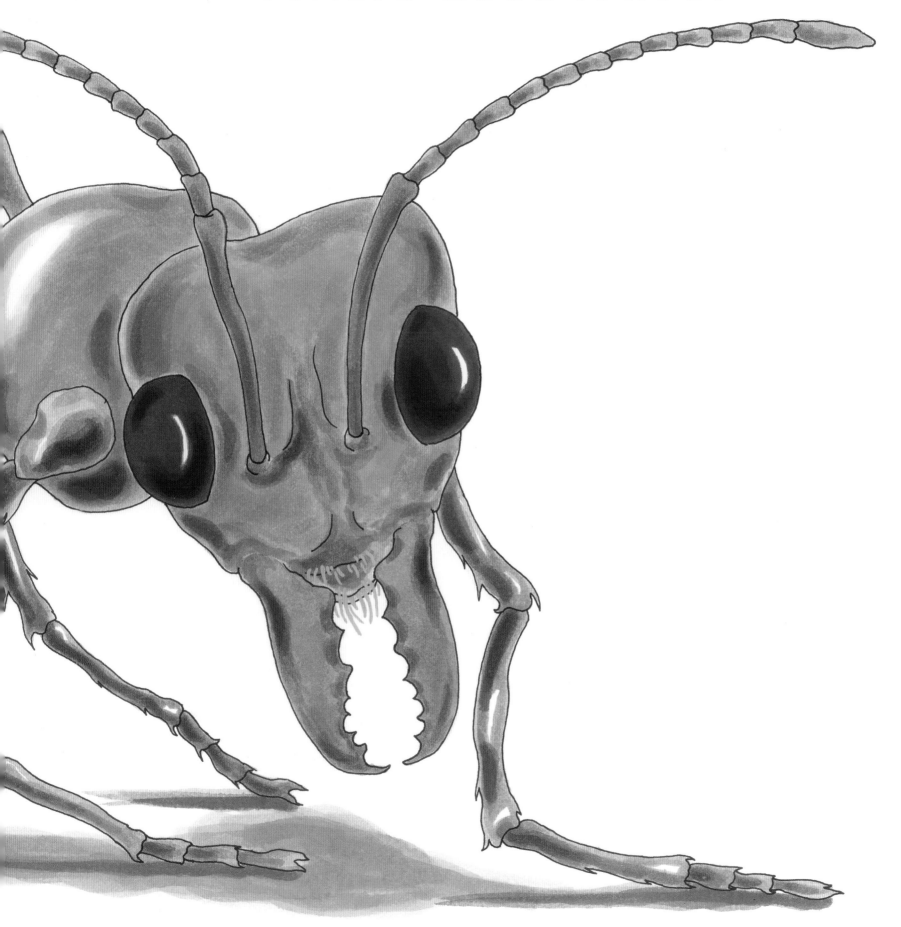

AUSTRALIAN WEAVER ANTS *(Oecophylla smaragdina)* build their nests, often in the shape of a large football, as a group effort. Worker ants gather in a line along the edge of a fresh green leaf. They grasp the edge of the leaf with their mandibles and pull with all their might until the edges join. If the edges are too far apart, the ants will form a chain, grasping the ant in front of them around the waist. Other ants complete the process by pasting the edges together with special silk glue. A nest is usually built in less than twenty-four hours. A colony may have several nests in the same tree or extend the nests to other trees. The big ants forage for food, build, and defend the colony, while the smaller ants stay home and care for the offspring.

This is a **Leaf-Cutter Bee.**

Where does it live?

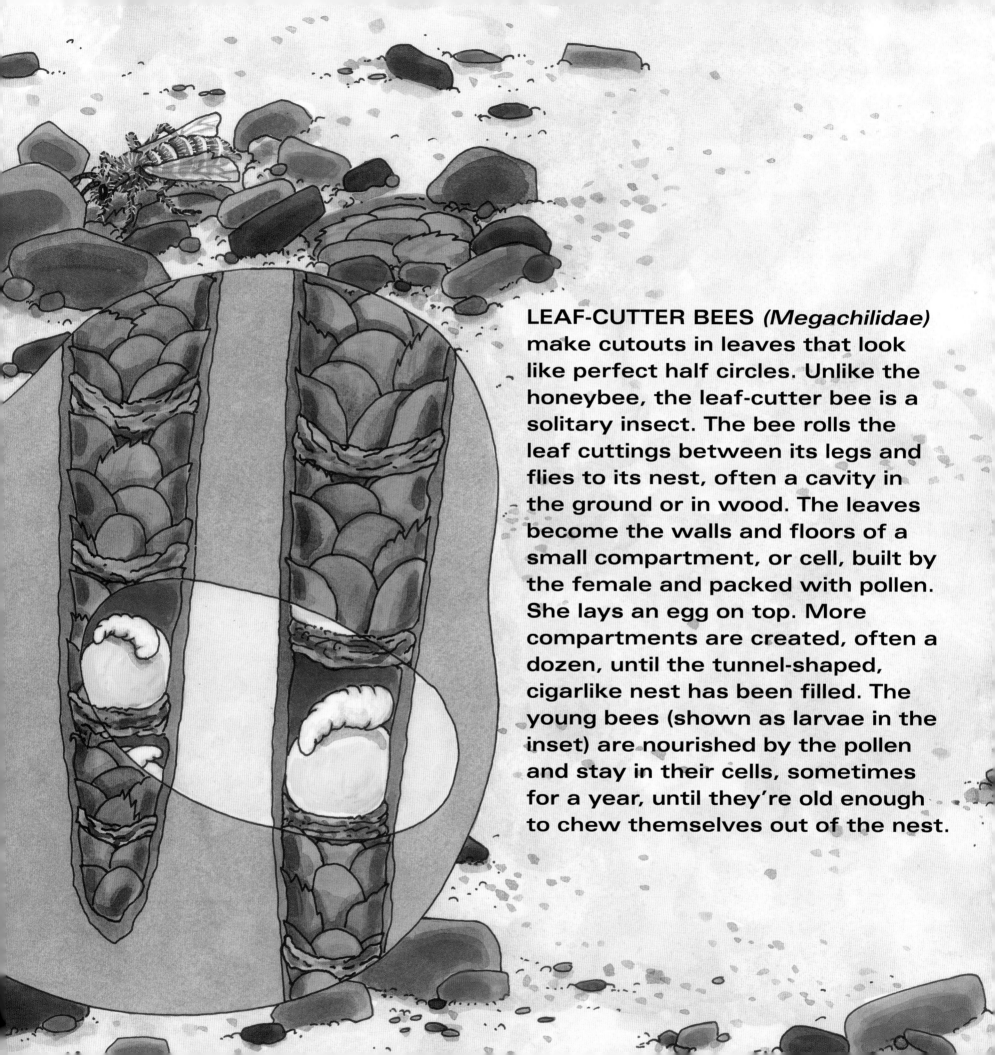

LEAF-CUTTER BEES (*Megachilidae*) make cutouts in leaves that look like perfect half circles. Unlike the honeybee, the leaf-cutter bee is a solitary insect. The bee rolls the leaf cuttings between its legs and flies to its nest, often a cavity in the ground or in wood. The leaves become the walls and floors of a small compartment, or cell, built by the female and packed with pollen. She lays an egg on top. More compartments are created, often a dozen, until the tunnel-shaped, cigarlike nest has been filled. The young bees (shown as larvae in the inset) are nourished by the pollen and stay in their cells, sometimes for a year, until they're old enough to chew themselves out of the nest.

This is a **Pine Processionary Caterpillar.**

Where does it live?

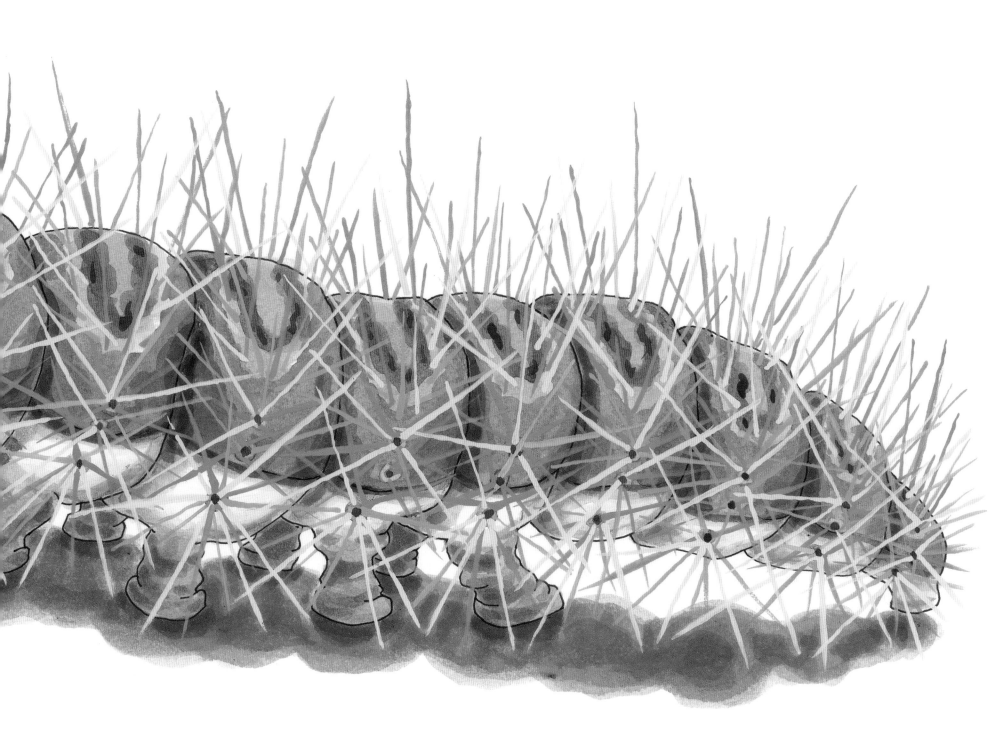

White and silky, the nest of a PINE PROCESSIONARY CATERPILLAR *(Thaumetopoea pityocampa)* looks like cotton candy. During the fall, the whole caterpillar family, as many as three hundred, builds the nest near the end of a pine branch. The branch is positioned to catch the rays of the sun, which keeps the nest warm throughout the winter. The caterpillars stay here all day. There's no definite opening—to leave the nest, the caterpillars force themselves through the silk. After sunset they go out in search of food, mainly pine needles. They follow their leader in an orderly procession, touching nose to tail—thousands of little legs moving in perfect unison. They return to the nest at dawn to rest and digest their food. In the spring, the caterpillars leave the nest and burrow into soft ground, emerging months later as moths.

This is an **African Termite**.

Where does it live?

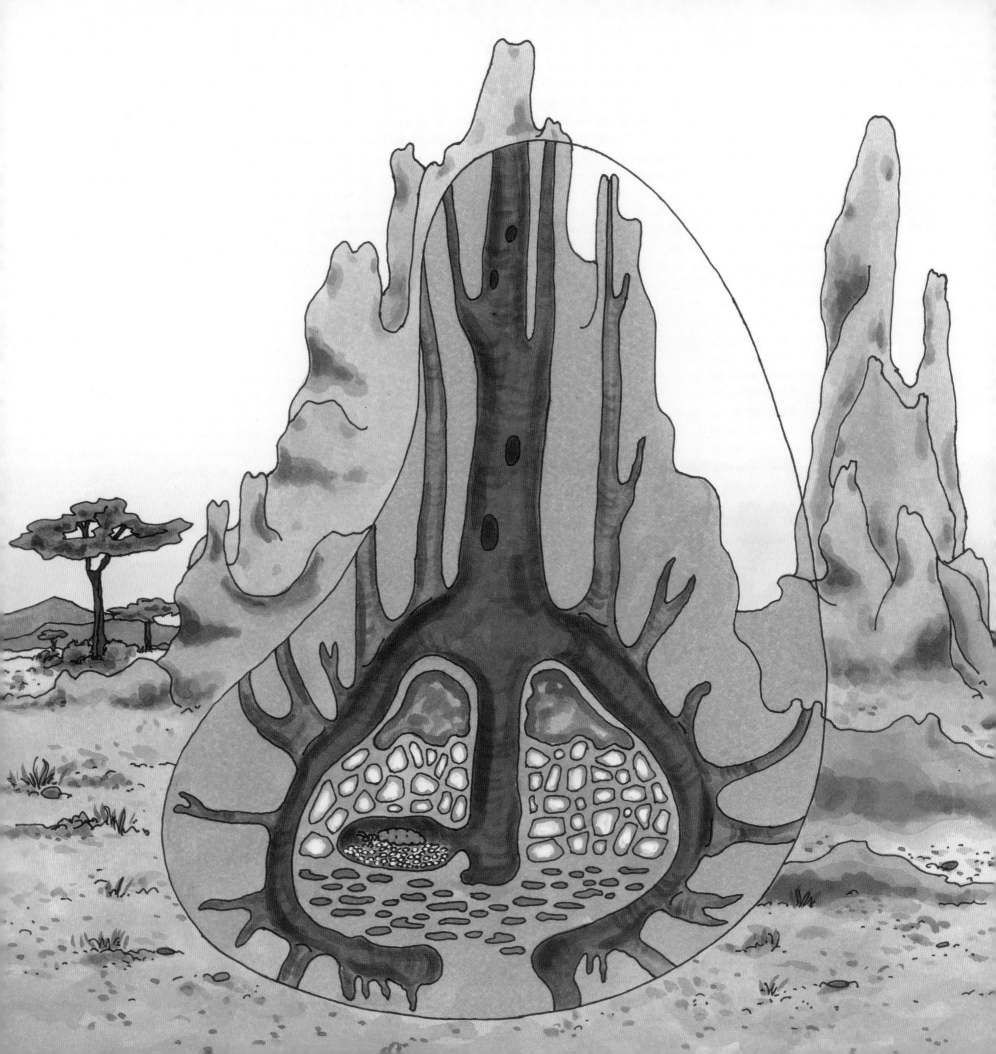

An **AFRICAN TERMITE** *(Macrotermes bellicosus)* home can rise higher than thirty feet (9 m). It is the tallest structure ever built relative to the size of the builder; to match it, humans would have to add almost a thousand feet (305 m) to what is now the world's tallest building. These termite mounds, which also extend underground, are an engineering masterpiece. One amazing feature is a ventilation system so sophisticated that it maintains a constant temperature of 84 to 86 degrees Fahrenheit (28–30°C) throughout the nest, no matter the weather. A termite mound houses as many as five million termites and includes a queen's chamber, larvae nurseries, and fungus gardens for food. The queen may live for fifteen years and lays all the eggs—up to one egg every three seconds. Some mounds have been used continuously by termites for hundreds, possibly thousands, of years.

This is a **Paper Hornet**.

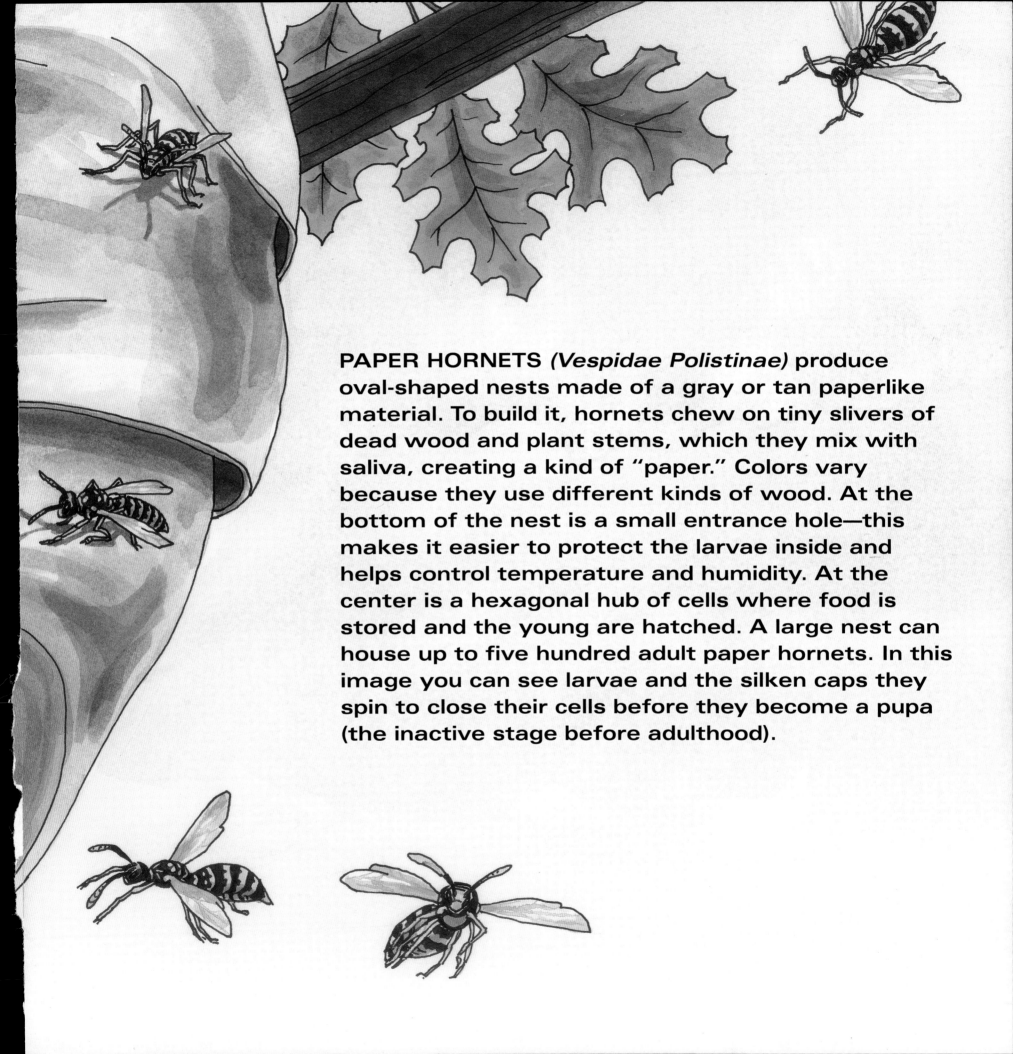

PAPER HORNETS *(Vespidae Polistinae)* produce oval-shaped nests made of a gray or tan paperlike material. To build it, hornets chew on tiny slivers of dead wood and plant stems, which they mix with saliva, creating a kind of "paper." Colors vary because they use different kinds of wood. At the bottom of the nest is a small entrance hole—this makes it easier to protect the larvae inside and helps control temperature and humidity. At the center is a hexagonal hub of cells where food is stored and the young are hatched. A large nest can house up to five hundred adult paper hornets. In this image you can see larvae and the silken caps they spin to close their cells before they become a pupa (the inactive stage before adulthood).

BUG WORDS

Abdomen: The rear part of an insect's body.

Antennae: Two long, thin "feelers" on a bug's head.

Arachnid: An arthropod with eight legs; a spider. Spiders are not technically "insects" because of their extra set of legs.

Arthropod: An invertebrate animal with jointed legs and a body divided into segments. Insects and spiders are arthropods.

Camouflage: Patterns or colors that help an animal blend into its surroundings and hide from predators.

Compound eyes: Eyes made up of smaller eyes or many lenses.

Insect: An arthropod with three main body parts: a head (with eyes and antennae), thorax (with wings and six legs), and an abdomen.

Invertebrate: An animal without a backbone. (Humans are vertebrates—we have a backbone.)

Larva: The stage when an insect is hatched from eggs; often the larva is wingless and wormlike.

Mandible: An insect's jaws.

Metamorphosis: The changes that an insect goes through as it grows—usually: egg, larva, pupa, and adult.

Pollen: Powder or grains made by a flower and carried by traveling insects.

Predator: A creature that hunts other animals for food.

Pupa: The stage when an insect is usually enclosed in a cocoon or protective covering and undergoes major growth changes.

Thorax: The middle part of an insect's body (including its wings and legs).

LEARN MORE ABOUT INSECTS AND SPIDERS

Books

Hillyard, Paul. *The Book of the Spider*. New York: Harper Perennial, 1998.

Hölldobler, Bert, and Wilson, Edward O. *Journey to the Ants: A Story of Scientific Exploration*. Cambridge, MA: Harvard University Press, 1998.

Kitchen, Bert. *And So They Build*. Cambridge, MA: Candlewick, 1993.

Koch, Maryjo. *Dragonfly Beetle Butterfly Bee*. New York: Smithmark Publishers, 1999.

Markle, Sandra. *Hornets: Incredible Insect Architects*. Minneapolis, MN: Lerner, 2008.

Mound, Laurence. *Insect*. New York: Dorling Kindersley, 2007.

O'Toole, Christopher. *The Encyclopedia of Insects*. New York: Facts on File, 1995.

Websites

University of Florida: Featured Creatures
http://entnemdept.ufl.edu/creatures/main/search_common.htm

Bug Bios
http://www.insects.org

Glossopedia